MISCARRIAGE GRIEF JOURNAL

48 Journaling Prompts to Process the Loss of a Baby

By Rachel J. Floyd

THIS JOURNAL IS IN MEMORY OF:

AGED:

DUE DATE:

THIS JOURNAL

Dear Reader,

First, I am so sorry for your loss. It must be so hard.

Second, this book is designed for you. This journal is designed to be a framework for you to process some of what you are feeling after experiencing the loss of a baby.

It is not meant to be a replacement for the support you may need from friends or family. Nor does it offer the same benefits that professional counseling offers. This book is not meant to give you the peace you may find from a higher power. But this book may compliment any or all of those things, or help when you just can't get support in those other areas, for whatever reason.

I wrote this book so that you know you are not alone. Your grief is unique, as are your specific experiences. Your story is worth exploring. The prompts are designed for you to reflect and crystalize some of what you are feeling. I hope you find safety in your journaling. I hope that through some of the prompts, that you begin to heal.

Grief is not something that can be neatly wrapped in a bow. By the end of this journal, you will still have your grief. But it is my hope that as you work through the following pages, your grief feels a little lighter.

With Love,
The Author

YOUR BABY

Take some time to write about your baby.

The first few prompts will help you reflect on your baby's life and the memories you will carry of them.

DATE:

How did it feel when you found out you were pregnant? Who did you tell first?

DATE:

How did you first find out you were pregnant?

DATE:

What were some things that you sensed about your baby when they were in utero?

_____

_____

_____

_____

_____

_____

_____

_____

_____

_____

_____

_____

_____

_____

_____

_____

_____

DATE:

What were some of your first hopes and dreams you had for your baby?

DATE:

What will you remember most about being pregnant?

DATE:

When I close my eyes and picture my baby, I see...

_____

_____

_____

_____

_____

_____

_____

_____

_____

_____

_____

_____

_____

_____

_____

_____

_____

DETAILS

Write about as many details of your miscarriage as you feel comfortable with. If there is a prompt that feels too hard to answer, skip it.

This journal is a safe space for you. You will write if and when you are ready. Remember, there are no right or wrong answers. Blank spaces are allowed.

DATE:

What were your initial feelings?

DATE:

How far along were you when you miscarried?

DATE:

Who did you tell first? Did you tell them right away?

DATE:

Describe your miscarriage process.

_____

_____

_____

_____

_____

_____

_____

_____

_____

_____

_____

_____

_____

_____

_____

_____

DATE:

I feel...

DATE:

My body feels...

_____

_____

_____

_____

_____

_____

_____

_____

_____

_____

_____

_____

_____

_____

_____

_____

_____

DATE:

Did you know the gender of the baby? Did they have a name?

DATE:

Is this your first miscarriage? If not, how has this differed from others?

RELATIONSHIPS

The next few prompts will help you to consider the support you have gotten from your partner, or what support has been lacking.

If you do not have a partner, you may choose to respond to the prompts as you feel. You may also choose to skip them.

DATE:

How did your partner first react to the miscarriage?

_____

_____

_____

_____

_____

_____

_____

_____

_____

_____

_____

_____

_____

_____

_____

_____

_____

DATE:

How has your partner given you support?

DATE:

How have you been able to support your partner?

_____

_____

_____

_____

_____

_____

_____

_____

_____

_____

_____

_____

_____

_____

_____

_____

_____

DATE:

How has your partner been throughout this process?

DATE:

How have they been grieving? How has that felt for you?

_____

_____

_____

_____

_____

_____

_____

_____

_____

_____

_____

_____

_____

_____

_____

_____

_____

_____

DATE:

What is something that you wish your partner understood?

DATE:

What have you and your partner talked about? What havent you talked about?

_____

_____

_____

_____

_____

_____

_____

_____

_____

_____

_____

_____

_____

_____

_____

_____

_____

_____

_____

_____

DATE:

What are your hopes and fears for you and your
partner as you move forward?

DATE:

Do you have other children? How have they been during this time?

_____

_____

_____

_____

_____

_____

_____

_____

_____

_____

_____

_____

_____

_____

_____

_____

_____

_____

DATE:

Write a letter to your partner:

YOUR FEELINGS

You. Your grief. No one knows exactly how you feel, but the next few pages are designed for you to help sort out your thoughts and feelings for your own purposes.

If you are not ready, you can always skip a page and come back later when it feels better. Your experiences are valid and you are allowed to feel exactly as you do.

This is your story.

DATE:

What do you feel angry about?

DATE:

What do you feel sad about?

DATE:

What do you feel curious about?

What has felt the most raw?

DATE:

Thoughts I know are not true but I can't help from thinking are:

DATE:

The thing I hate to admit most is:

_____

_____

_____

_____

_____

_____

_____

_____

_____

_____

_____

_____

_____

_____

_____

_____

_____

_____

DATE:

The hardest part emotionally has been:

DATE:

How did you initially feel? How do you feel now?

DATE:

What have you been doing to heal?

_____
_____
_____
_____
_____
_____
_____
_____
_____
_____
_____
_____
_____
_____
_____
_____
_____

DATE:

Where have you found small moments of joy?

_____

_____

_____

_____

_____

_____

_____

_____

_____

_____

_____

_____

_____

_____

_____

_____

DATE:

How have you been reorienting yourself? Where do
you go from here?

DATE:

Write a letter to your baby.

AFTERWARD

In the days and weeks that followed your loss, you have continued to keep going.

This section will help you reflect on the events after your miscarriage and your emotions surrounding them.

DATE:

My most trusted people throughout this has been:

_____

_____

_____

_____

_____

_____

_____

_____

_____

_____

_____

_____

_____

_____

_____

_____

DATE:

Did you recieve any hurtful comments from friends
or family after you told them about the miscarriage?

DATE:

What has given you hope during this season of life?

DATE:

What gives you comfort?

DATE:

How have you felt healing? What activities feel soul soothing?

DATE:

What kindness were you shown during this time?
Who has shown you love?

DATE:

What are some comforting words that you have found meaning in?

_____

_____

_____

_____

_____

_____

_____

_____

_____

_____

_____

_____

_____

_____

_____

_____

_____

DATE:

What do you feel angry about?

DATE:

What are you grateful for?

DATE:

What are some songs or artists that you have been listening to a lot lately? Do any specific lines stand out to you?

DATE:

What other resorces have felt helpful, even if only a little?

_____

_____

_____

_____

_____

_____

_____

_____

_____

_____

_____

_____

_____

_____

_____

_____

_____

_____

DATE:

Write a letter to yourself.

NOTES:

If you need more space to finish any prompts or just need to answer your own questions, continue writing here.

Printed in Great Britain
by Amazon

35533020R00058